Quality Assurance Guide

How to Set Up and Manage a Quality Control System

By Meir Liraz

(Including 10 Special Bonuses)

Published by Liraz Publishing

www.BizMove.com

Copyright © Liraz Publishing. All rights reserved.

ISBN: 9781695421431

Table of Contents

1. Basic Quality Elements — 5
2. A Sample Manual — 7
3. Scope - 1.0 — 9
4. Responsibilities - 2.0 — 10
5. Purchase Order Control - 3.0 — 12
6. Drawing and Specification Change Control - 4.0 — 13
7. Receiving Inspection - 5.0 — 14
8. Raw Material Control - 6.0 — 16
9. In Process Inspection - 7.0
10. Assembly Inspection and Functional Testing - 8.0 — 20
11. Final Inspection and Testing - 9.0 — 22
12. Faulty (Discrepant) Material Control - 10.0
13. Tool and Gage Control - 11.0 — 27
14. Overrun Stock Control - 12.0 — 28
15. Packing and Shipping - 13.0 — 29

Supplements:

16. How to Increases Productivity in Your Business — 40
17. The Equipment Replacement Decision — 55
18. Fixing Production Mistakes — 70

Appendix: Special Free Bonuses

MEIR LIRAZ

1. Basic Quality Elements

This guide presents a sample quality control system closely prepared from one developed by a fortune 500 company. It may be used as a guide in initiating your own quality assurance system, whether you sell to consumers, industrial users, or government.

All quality and inspection systems have simple, basic elements in common:

Organization - setting and assigning specific authority and responsibility for each phase of the system;

Quality Planning - writing work instructions with realistic "defect prevention" rules, looking at manufacturing processes for possible quality trouble spots, setting acceptance/rejection standards, controlling accepted/rejected products, and setting up a means of using suppliers' and customers' failure information to improve product quality;

Product Specification Control - making sure everyone always has the latest technical data for properly producing, inspecting, and shipping the product;

Supplier Product Quality Control - watching

purchases to make sure that the people you buy from know and observe your quality requirements as well as technical specifications;

Measurement and Test Equipment Control - setting up a system to insure that such equipment is properly and regularly calibrated to established standards;

Nonconforming Material Control - spotting defects as early in production as possible and keeping faulty items from reaching customers; and

Records and Reports - setting up a system that tracks all steps of the production, inspection, and shipping cycle to identity existing and potential problem areas.

The following sample manual incorporates these basics. It may be adapted to fit your needs. It is recommended that each section of a manual you work up be on a loose-leaf sheet for easy reference and revision. Remember, the best manual in the world won't do any good unless every employee - not just those in Quality Assurance - is convinced that producing quality products is of prime importance.

QUALITY ASSURANCE GUIDE

2. A Sample Manual

Introduction

This manual describes for our employees and customers our quality control system. The system applies both to the items we produce and to the items we buy from our suppliers.

As dictated by the complexity of product design, manufacturing techniques used, and customer requirements, more specific written procedures may be required to implement the policies set in this manual.

No changes may be made to this manual or any supplementary quality control procedures unless approved by the plant manager or an authorized representative.

Table of Contents

Description / Section

Scope - 1.0

Responsibilities - 2.0

Purchase Order Control - 3.0

Drawing and Specification Change Control - 4.0

MEIR LIRAZ

Receiving Inspection - 5.0

Raw Material Control - 6.0

In Process Inspection - 7.0

Assembly Inspection and Functional Testing - 8.0

Final Inspection and Testing - 9.0

Faulty (Discrepant) Material Control - 10.0

Tool and Gage Control - 11.0

Overrun Stock Control - 12.0

Packing and Shipping - 13.0

Identification - 4.0

Appendix A Organization Chart -

Appendix B Purchase Order Form

Appendix C Inspection Data Form -

(Each company should use its own forms for the Appendices).

Appendix D Identification Tags

Appendix E Travel Card

1.0 Scope

1.1 The quality control system includes: receiving, identifying, stocking and issuing parts and material; all manufacturing processes; packing, storing; and shipping.

1.2 The system is designed to ensure customer satisfaction through quality control management of supplies made and services performed here, and by our suppliers at their facilities. It is designed to spot processing problems early so we can correct them before we've produced a lot of faulty items.

1.3 Written inspection and test procedures will be prepared to supplement drawings and other specifications, as necessary.

2.0 Responsibilities

2.1 The supervisor of quality assurance reports directly to the plant manager.

2.2 The quality assurance supervisor's responsibilities include:

2.2.1 Planning how to meet customer's quality requirements

2.2.2 Reviewing customer drawings and specifications.

2.2.3 Determining inspection points.

2.2.4 Writing inspection and test instructions.

2.2.5 Establishing (and making sure employees follow) the most effective and efficient quality assurance procedures possible.

2.2.6 Keeping adequate quality assurance records.

2.2.7 Reviewing quality assurance records and overseeing follow-up for correction and prevention of defects.

2.2.8 Assuring that our suppliers' quality control and follow-up are adequate.

2.2.9 Inspecting all special and standard gages, test equipment, and tooling used to manufacture products when we acquire them and calibrating them on a regularly scheduled basis.

2.2.10 Coordinating in-plant correction of items rejected by customers, explaining to customers what action will be taken, and evaluating the actions for effectiveness.

2.2.11 Making sure inspectors make unbiased decisions to accept or reject items.

3.0 Purchase Order Control

3.1 All of our purchase orders to suppliers must be approved by the plant manager or an authorized representative.

3.2 When the purchase order is released, our buyer will send our supplier all required drawings, specifications, and other customer requirements (such as material or process certifications, physical or chemical analysis, source inspections) with the purchase order.

3.3 If there is a drawing or specification change after our order is placed with the supplier, our buyer will send the supplier a purchase order change, including our latest Engineering change and the latest drawings or other specifications.

3.4 Copies of all purchase orders will be kept on file for our customers to review.

4.0 Drawing and Specification Change Control

4.1 We manufacture to customer drawings and specifications. Sets of these are filed in job number folders in Production Control files.

4.2 Production Control is responsible for charging out and keeping track of drawings and specifications.

4.3 The Sales Department receives Engineering changes from our customers and is responsible for sending these changes to Production Control immediately.

4.4 Production Control is responsible for issuing the latest Engineering changes, drawings, and specifications of departments that need them and for voiding outdated Engineering changes, drawings, and specifications.

4.5 A standard procedure will be set up to control changes by effective date or serial/lot number.

5.0 Receiving Inspection

5.1 All parts and materials will be received and logged in by the Receiving Department.

5.2 All parts and materials will be sent to Receiving Inspection after logging in.

5.3 Receiving Inspection will assure that proper certification, physical and chemical test data, special process certifications, or source inspection certifications are with the items to be inspected.

5.4 The receiving inspector must document the complete results of all inspection and tests.

5.5 Inspection will identify accepted lots and send them to stock.

5.6 Rejected lots will be identified and set aside in Receiving Inspection until the buyer and Production Control decide on disposition.

5.7 The Receiving Department will send a copy of each rejection report to the Purchasing Department and the supplier.

5.8 The Purchasing Department has the responsibility of assuring that a pattern of continually receiving faulty items from any supplier doesn't develop and assuring supplier corrective action.

5.9 The Quality Department will follow-up to see that a supplier who has sent us items we reject has effectively corrected what it has been doing wrong.

5.10 Receiving Inspection instructions will be written with consideration given to the complexity of the parts, material received, and customer requirements. Follow customer instructions (if any) for inspection.

5.11 Sample according to customer requirements (if any).

5.12 The Quality Department will review Receiving Inspection records periodically to see if any suppliers are consistently failing to meet standards.

5.13 All inspection records will show the number inspected, the number rejected, and the name of the inspector.

5.14 Inspection records will also show the disposition of supplier-provided records and data.

6.0 Raw Material Control

6.1 Raw materials, bar stock, sheet stock, and castings will be marked so they can be traced to their certification, and stored in an area apart from the normal flow of in-process material.

6.2 Copies of all certifications will be filed in the job order number folder by job order number and available for customer review.

6.3 Only raw material accepted by Receiving Inspection will be released for production.

6.4 Certified stock will be issued from its storage area only for job order requirements.

6.5 Verification of suppliers' certifications will be ordered from independent testing laboratories when deemed necessary by the Quality Department or to meet our customers' requirements.

6.6 All certifications will be traceable to purchase order, date of receipt of the material, and the inspector of the material.

QUALITY ASSURANCE GUIDE

In Process Inspection

7.1 The Quality Department will make first piece inspection after set up is completed and approved by Production.

7.2 No production runs will be made until first piece inspection is accepted.

7.3 After first piece inspection acceptance, in-process inspections will be made by the Quality Department at intervals adequate for early detection of processes producing material that doesn't meet standards.

7.4 The Quality Department will keep records of all first   piece and in-process inspections.

7.5 The inspection records will be stored in the job number folder and will be available for customer review.

7.6 Tag or otherwise identify rejected items and move them to an area apart from the normal flow of in-process materials.

7.7 The Quality Department will follow-up to prevent recurrence of faulty material.

7.8 Inspection records will list: the number of

pieces accepted, the number rejected, kind of defects and basic causes of rejection, date of inspection, and the inspector's name.

7.9 Attachment shows the locations of fabrication and inspection stations. For each station, it lists the types of items subject to inspection, the kind of inspection done, and the applicable drawings and specifications.

7.10 Special processes will require appropriate inspections and controls, including qualification and certification of personnel and equipment.

8.0 Assembly Inspection and Functional Testing

8.1 Production personnel will make assembly inspections and do functional testing, as required.

8.2 The Quality Department will check functional test under an established sampling plan.

8.3 The Quality Department will keep the inspection records.

8.4 The inspection records will be kept in the job number folder and will be available for customer review.

8.5 All faulty (discrepant) assemblies will be marked and set apart so they won't be accidentally used.

8.6 The Quality Department will initiate corrective and follow-up action to prevent recurrence of faulty material.

8.7 Inspection records will list: the number accepted, the number rejected, the date of the inspection, and the inspector's name.

9.0 Final inspection and Testing

9.1 Final inspection and tests will be performed either on 100 percent or on a sample of the items. The number of items sampled will depend on the complexity of the items and customer requirements. Inspection will follow either customer-supplied procedures when available or MIL-STD-105D.

9.2 Each end item will be inspected/tested 100 percent, unless the customer asks otherwise.

9.3 The Quality Department will keep all final inspection and test records.

9.4 Inspection and test records will be filed in the job number folder and will be available for customer review,

9.5 The Quality Department will follow-up to see that processes producing faulty materials are corrected and to prevent recurrence of faulty material from those processes.

9.6 All faulty material will be marked and set apart from the normal flow of finished material.

9.7 Faulty material will not be shipped to the customer without specific customer instructions to submit such Nonconforming material.

9.8 Rejected material which has been repaired, reworked, or sorted must be resubmitted to final inspection to make sure it meets requirements.

9.9 Inspection records will list: the number of pieces accepted, the number rejected, the date of inspection; and the inspector's name.

10.0 Faulty (Discrepant) Material Control

10.1 All faulty (Nonconforming) material, supplies, or parts will be placed in a "DO NOT USE" area. The items will be clearly marked with job number, part number, revision letter, lot size, defect, inspector's name, and any other information necessary.

10.2 The specific reason an item has been rejected will be clearly written on a rejection tag attached to each part or container.

10.3 No one may remove items from the "DO NOT USE" area until disposition is determined by a Material Review Board made up of the plant manager, and representatives of the Production and Quality Departments.

10.4 Nonconforming material will not be shipped unless the customer's buyer approves it. The shipping documents will be marked with what's wrong with the items.

10.5 The Quality Department will control all lots submitted for acceptance inspection. Each lot will be kept as a unit, apart from other lots, and out of the normal flow of material.

10.6 During the processing of material all production and inspection operations must be kept in proper order. Each step must be completed before the next step is begun.

10.7 The Quality Department will set up a system so that the stage of inspection each item is in, can easily be identified.

10.8 Unidentified material will be taken out of the normal flow of production until it is inspected to insure that it meets all specifications.

10.9 Reworked material will be segregated from other material until the Quality Department determines its status.

11.0 Tool and Gage Control

11.1 All special tools, jigs, fixtures, gages, and measuring equipment must be properly identified,

11.2 Each new or reworked tool, jig, fixture, gage, and item of measuring equipment will be inspected before issue for use.

11.3 All gages, measuring and test equipment will be calibrated to standards.

11.4 A written schedule for calibrating gages, measuring and test equipment will be set and strictly followed. Frequency of calibration will be based on type and purpose of the equipment and severity of usage.

11.5 A restricted area for storing and calibrating gages, measuring, and test equipment will be set up.

11.5.1 A strict system of issue, control, and return will be set and followed.

11.6 If the customer supplies special gages, they will be checked at the intervals the customer sets. If the customer supplies no inspection schedule, the equipment will be checked according to a schedule that takes into account type, purpose, and severity of use.

11.7 Calibration will follow the written procedures kept in the calibration area.

11.8 Obsolete or out-of service tools and gages will be tagged.

11.9 Decals or stickers will be put on tools and gages or their containers to show the last date of calibration and the due date of the next calibration.

11.10 Personal, as well as company-0wned production and inspection tools, must be properly and regularly calibrated.

12.0 Overrun Stock Control

12.1 The Quality Department will oversee overrun stock.

12.2 The Quality Department will insure that any overrun parts sent to stock are properly marked "accepted." The part number, latest drawing number and specification revision, date of inspection, job number, and quantity of parts will be shown. The Quality Department will periodically check to see that the parts are properly packed to prevent deterioration and damage.

12.3 No overrun parts will be shipped to a customer until they are reinspected and found in acceptable condition and to meet the latest drawing and specification revisions.

13.0 Packing and Shipping

13.1 No order will be shipped to a customer until all shipping papers are stamped or signed and dated by the final inspector.

13.2 No order will be shipped until all required certifications, test reports, special samples, etc., have been packed with the material in accordance with the customer's requirements and accepted by the final inspector.

13.3 All material will be packed to prevent damage deterioration, and substitution.

13.4 The customer will be identified on the packaging, parts, and as otherwise necessary to prevent lost and misdirected shipments.

13.5 The order will be packed as directed by the customer, if applicable.

14.0 Identification

14.1 All materials and articles will be identified by a basic part number and revision letter.

14.2 Critical materials and articles will also carry a serial or lot number. If required, a list of materials and articles by identification numbers will be attached.

16. How to Increase the Productivity in Your Business

The aim of this productivity management guide is to provide small business owners and managers with an overview of how company productivity can be improved. It covers what productivity is, how it is measured, and what a company can do to increase it.

Why should productivity management growth be a national concern? It is because, if too low, the Nation can neither improve its standard of living at home nor compete successfully abroad. Productivity growth affects wage negotiations, inflation rates, business decisions, exchange rates, a host of other economic, political and social conditions, and, therefore, every small business owner and manager.

The factors affecting both National and individual firm productivity are many and diverse. Nationally, changes in employment, hours worked, the educational, age and sex composition of the work force, levels of capital investment and savings, government regulations, capacity utilization, inflation, among others, all can affect, favorably or unfavorably, productivity rates.

There are many productivity factors the firm can manage. How well does the firm utilize new knowledge; is it working at an economy-of-scale level; are the employees highly motivated and loyal or is there labor unrest and high worker turnover; is the resource (human and capital) allocation maximizing established goals; and finally, what is the overall quality of the company's management? And, if management sees productivity as a problem, is there a commitment to establish a company-wide Productivity Improvement Program?

Establishing A Productivity Improvement Program

Recent studies indicate that the quality of management is the key to increasing business productivity. It is up to the managers to identify productivity problems and develop an appropriate program to solve these problems. In the past several years, many of the Nation's most successful, larger corporations have started Productivity improvement Programs (PIP). With profits slipping, their managements realized that improving productivity was the key to improving income; that only through an efficient and effective utilization of resources could they remain competitive and profitable.

The following Productivity Improvement Program outlines the key elements of programs successfully used by many companies including such giants as Honeywell, Westinghouse, GM and Ford.

Key elements of a Productivity Improvement Program (PIP):

1. Obtain Upper Management Support. Without top management support, experience shows a PIP likely will fail. The Chief Executive Officer should issue a clear, comprehensive policy statement. The statement should be communicated to everyone in the company. Top management also must be willing to allocate adequate resources to permit success.

2. Create New Organizational Components. A Steering Committee to oversee the PIP and Productivity Managers to implement it are essential. The Committee should be staffed by top departmental executives with the responsibilities of goal setting, guidance, advice, and general control. The Productivity Managers are responsible for the day-to-day activities of measurement and analysis.

The responsibilities of all organizational components must be clear and well established.

3. Plan Systematically. Success doesn't just happen. Goals and objectives should be set, problems targeted and rank ordered, reporting and monitoring requirements developed, and feedback channels established.

4. Open Communications. Increasing productivity means changing the way things are done. Desired changes must be communicated. Communication should flow up and down the business organization. Through publications, meetings, and films, employees must be told what is going on and how they will benefit.

5. Involve Employees. This is a very broad element encompassing the quality of work life, worker motivation, training, worker attitudes, job enrichment, quality circles, incentive systems and much more. Studies show a characteristic of successful, growing businesses is that they develop a "corporate culture" where employees strongly identify with and are an important part of company life. This sense of belonging is not easy to engender. Through basic fairness, employee involvement, and

equitable incentives, the corporate culture and productivity both can grow.

6. Measure and Analyze. This is the technical key to success for a PIP. Productivity must be defined, formulas and worksheets developed, sources of data identified, benchmark studies performed, and personnel assigned. Measuring productivity can be a highly complex task. The goal, however, is to keep it as simple as possible without distorting and depreciating the data. Measurement is so critical to success, a more detailed analysis is helpful.

Measuring Productivity

In an informal sense, productivity is getting more bang for the buck or doing the right things right. But these definitions do not help much when actual measurement is required. For that, a more mathematical approach is needed.

Productivity is a ratio, a comparison of what is produced and what is used to produce it. It compares outputs with inputs, that is, it divides outputs by inputs. Output is a physical entity - a car, a lightbulb, a typed page, or a processed pay voucher. For measurement, an output must be countable over time, a direct result of identifiable activities, and homogeneous (don't mix apples and oranges). Inputs can be classified into four types: labor, materials, capital and energy.

Each input can be used as the basis of a partial measure of productivity, depending upon circumstances. Labor productivity, for example, is measured by dividing output by hours worked, number of employees, or labor cost. Capital productivity is arrived at by dividing output by money invested or machine hours used. Materials productivity is output divided by units of materials used, units of scrap, or money spent. And energy productivity is output divided by units of energy consumed (like BTU's), or money spent.

Labor productivity (output = hours worked) is used by the government as the measure of the Nation's productivity. Many large, diversified companies, however, now use all four inputs to determine what is called Total Factor Productivity. In a purely office environment, since labor is the key input, some organizations use what is called the Administrative Productivity Index (API). It divides work output such as typing, loans serviced, clients interviewed or invoices processed by total hours worked to produce the administrative output. So the API essentially is a labor productivity measure.

Outputs and inputs can be measured in physical units or values or both. For example, an input unit for labor is hours and for value is dollars. A unit of output is the physical count of something and its value is its base selling price. If value (the dollar) is used as the basis of measurement, inflation must be accounted for to maintain a true value over time in constant dollars. Thus, all input and output values usually are tied to the Producer Price Index of each input and output (this compensates for the impact of inflation) to maintain valid input-output and value relationships in constant dollars over time. In other words, if revenues from product A increased 20% over last year, but its price increased by 8% to account for inflation, the real increase in dollar output was 12%. Yearly comparisons must be done using constant dollars. If the company mixes dollars and units, it still must deflate the dollars to maintain a valid relationship between physical quantities and value.

Another complicating aspect of measuring productivity is that not all inputs are equal and not all outputs are the same. Some production processes are more labor intensive than others;

some use a variety of different labor skill (value) levels. Output products also change in quality and composition over time. So the process of weighing inputs and outputs to account for their relative values must be done before a truly accurate productivity measure is possible.

The point to remember is, whether employing a partial or total productivity measurement, whether for service or industrial application, or whether the business is large or small, all inputs and outputs must reflect constant values and true mixtures. To do this, all factors must be deflated and weighed.

One final technical consideration, productivity measurements should be indexed to facilitate comparison. Index each input and output measure to a base year and assign each measure the number 100. This makes it easier to calculate percentage changes over time.

Measuring productivity is time consuming and demanding: inputs and outputs must be defined, appropriate formulas developed, worksheets for keeping count printed, data collected, and calculations made. But the result will be more than just some numbers. Productivity measurement will provide a tool to assess the efficiency and effectiveness of the company, to forecast investment requirements, and to estimate the impact of cost increases or technological advances. The results do justify the effort required.

Industry Examples

So much for theory and mechanics. In practice, how have various businesses and industries actually gone about improving productivity? In the banking industry, for example, there has been revolution in productivity in the past decade. Through the use of computers, magnetic ink character recognition equipment, and mechanizing various repetitive operations, there has been a 50 percent reduction in labor requirements for check handling between.

Studies on the cosmetics industry show that through improved technology and by utilizing larger plants, it maintained a solid 4% annual manufacturing productivity increase. Economies-ofscale seem to have been the key factor here since plants with 500 or more employees were 37% more productive than the smaller ones. Studies on administrative productivity programs indicate that improved productivity comes from standardizing administrative procedures, streamlining operations, and increasing computer applications. These examples illustrate the importance to productivity of both advanced technology and proper management.

Different businesses use different measures of productivity. Airlines traditionally have used passengers boarded per employee and revenue tonmiles per employee as partial productivity measures. The Bell System has developed a sophisticated productivity program and integrated it into its overall budgeting and planning activities. The Bell program is worth a closer look.

Bell uses two Partial Productivity measures-volume of business per employee and number of phones served per employee. Both measure labor productivity. Bell also uses three Total Factor Productivity (TFP) measures to determine overall corporate performance.

One TFP measure emphasizes total output, the others gross and net value added.

Bell's TFP inputs are capital, labor, and materials. All are reported in current dollars, deflated, weighed, averaged, and indexed to arrive at a single

Total Input Index. Because of the great variety of Bell products and services, output is measured in current revenues, not physical units. Again, the revenue dollars are deflated. All categories of revenues are then summed to arrive at a total dollar output figure. That total is indexed to arrive at a single Total Output Index. Finally, the output index number is divided by the input index number and the resulting figure is the Total Factor Productivity Index for the company. The percentage change over time in the TFP Index is Bell's key measure of the entire company's productivity.

Bell uses this TFP model to track productivity trends, to compare them with industry norms, and to plan long term. They also combine productivity with traditional financial analysis to determine the impact on net income of productivity growth, price change, and many other variables.

A wide-range of businesses, from small to the Bell System, have implemented successful productivity programs. Their experiences have shown that effective programs are thoroughly planned, technically correct, and fully communicated.

17. The Equipment Replacement Decision

The parts replacement decision, to replace a piece of equipment should be based on facts and figures. The judgment which the owner-manager of a small company makes should be the result of weighing the costs of keeping the old equipment against the cost of its replacement.

This parts replacement guide discusses the elements involved in making such a cost comparison. Examples are used to illustrate the gathering and use of the appropriate cost figures.

Sooner or later, you must decide whether you should keep an existing unit of equipment or replace it with a new unit. As time goes by, equipment deteriorates and becomes obsolete. Frequent breakdowns occur, defective output increases, unit labor costs rise, and production schedules cannot be met. At some point, these occurrences become serious enough to cause you to wonder whether or not you should replace the equipment.

The problem is that the new equipment costs money, and the question that comes to you is: Will the advantages of the new equipment be great enough to justify the investment it requires?

You answer this question by making a cost comparison.

To recognize the better alternative you need to know the total cost of each alternative - keeping the old equipment or buying a replacement. Once these costs are determined, you can compare them and identify the more economical equipment. The paragraphs that follow discuss the individual costs which you must consider when computing the total cost of the old and new equipment.

Depreciation

One of the costs connected with any type of equipment is depreciation. For cost comparison purposes, depreciation is simply the amount by which an asset decreases in value over some period of time. For example, if you bought a piece of equipment for $20,000 and sold it for $6,000 after seven years of service, you would say that the depreciation during the seven-year period was $20,000 minus $6,000, or $14,000. This $14,000 was one of your costs of owning the equipment for that period.

From this, it follows that when considering equipment replacement, you must calculate the future depreciation expense that you will experience with both the old and the new equipment.

Insofar as the new equipment is concerned, this calls for knowing certain things about the equipment. You need to know (1) its first cost, (2) its estimated service life, and (3) its expected salvage value. The difference between the first cost and the salvage value will represent the amount by which the equipment will depreciate during its life - that is, during the time you expect to use it.

You determine the depreciation expense for the old equipment in the same general way but for one import difference. The difference is that no expenditure is required to procure the equipment because you already own it. However, a decision to keep it does require an investment at the present time. This investment is equal to the asset's market value - that is, to the amount of money the asset would bring in if it were replaced and sold. If this amount is not equal to the equipment's book value. the depreciation expense that was shown for accounting purposes is in error because it did not reflect the actual depreciation.

So to determine the actual future depreciation expense that will be experienced with the old equipment, you must know (1) its present market value, (2) its estimated remaining service life, and (3) its expected salvage value at the end of that life. The difference between the present market value and the future salvage value represents the amount by which the equipment will depreciate during its remaining life in your business.

To sum up, you must begin your cost comparison by determining the first cost of the new equipment and estimating its service life and salvage value. Also, you must determine the market value of the old equipment and estimate its remaining service life and future salvage value.

Interest

In addition to depreciation, every piece of equipment generates an interest expense. This expense occurs because owning an asset ties up some of your capital. If you had to borrow this capital you would have to pay for the use of the money. This "out-of-pocket" cost is one of the costs of owning the equipment.

The story is the same even when you use your own

money. In this case, the amount involved is no longer available for other investments which could bring you a return. This "opportunity cost" is one of the costs of owning the equipment.

To cite an example, suppose that the market value of an asset during a given year is $10,000. Suppose also that at the same time, you are getting capital at a cost of 15 percent per year. On the other hand, suppose that if you converted the asset into cash, you could invest the money and realize a rate of return of 15 percent per year. In either case, a decision to own that asset during that year would be costing you 15 percent of $10,000, or $1,500 in interest.

Thus, in any comparison of equipment alternatives, you must take the cost of money into account. So, when determining whether or not existing equipment should be replaced, you must estimate what money is costing you in terms of a percent per year.

Operating Costs

There is a third type of cost - the cost of operation - that is experienced with a piece of equipment. Typical operating cost are expenditures for labor, materials, supervision, maintenance, and power.

These cost must be considered because your choice of equipment affects them. You may find it convenient to estimate these costs on an annual basis. You can get figures for each unit of equipment by estimating its next-year operating costs as well as the annual rate at which these costs are likely to increase as wage rates rise and the equipment deteriorates.

For example, you might say that operating cost for the new equipment are likely to be $16,000 during the first year of its life. You might also estimate that after the first year, the operating costs will increase at a rate of $500 a year.

You can simplify the problem of estimating these costs by either (1) ignoring those costs that are the same for the old and the new equipment or (2) estimating only the differences between the operating costs of the two units. With this simplification, the total costs which you calculate for each type of equipment will be understated by the same amount. Therefore, the difference between these total costs will remain the same, and you will still be able to recognize the more economical alternative.

Revenues

Often, the revenues generated by the old and the new equipment will be the same. When this is true, revenues can be ignored for the same reason that you can ignore equal operating costs.

But if revenues are affected by the choice of equipment, they must be considered. For example, you might estimate that the higher quality of output from the new equipment will increase annual sales by $1,200. You can handle this difference in revenues in either of two ways.

One way is to show the $1,200 as an additional annual cost that will be experienced with the old equipment.

The other way is to treat the $1,200 as a negative annual cost and associate it with the new equipment. The total cost which you calculate will be affected by your choice of method, but the difference between these cost will remain the same.

An Annual Average Cost

In brief, you can make the necessary cost analysis

on the new and old equipment only after you have the proper data for each. For the new equipment, the data include first cost, service life, salvage value, operating costs, and revenue advantage. For the old equipment, the data include market value, remaining service life, future salvage value, and operating costs. In addition, for both alternatives, the cost of money must be stated in the form of an interest rate.

By using these data, you can determine the elements of the total costs. These elements consist of depreciation expense, interest expense, operating costs, and possibly lost revenues. Now, it so happens that these costs can be expressed in a variety of ways.

However, the simplest way for cost comparison purposes is to describe these cost elements in terms of an average annual cost. Doing so permits you to calculate and compare the total average annual costs of the old and new equipment and reach a decision.

How these costs can be computed is shown in the example that follows.

The Old Equipment

Look first at some facts about an old piece of equipment. It has a market value of $7,000. If retained, its service life is expected to be four years, and its salvage value is expected to be $1,000. Next-year operating costs are estimated to be $8,000 but will probably increase at an annual rate of $200. The cost of money is 12 percent per year. With this set of figures, you can obtain the total average annual cost of the alternative of keeping this equipment.

Annual Depreciation Expense. You begin by calculating the equipment's average annual depreciation expense. You do this by determining the total depreciation and dividing that amount by the asset's four-year life. Your answer is $1,500 which you get as follows:

Annual depreciation =

$$\frac{\$7{,}000 - \$1{,}000}{4} = \$1{,}500$$

Annual Interest Expense. Next, you calculate the average annual interest expense. The maximum investment in the equipment is $7,000, its present market value. But as time goes by, the investment in the asset decreases because its market value decreases. The minimum investment is reached at the end of the equipment's life when it has a salvage value of $1,000. The average investment will be the average of these maximum and minimum values. You calculate it as follows:

Average investment =

$$\frac{\$7,000 + \$1,000}{2} = \$4,000$$

To determine the average annual interest expense, you multiply the average investment ($4,000, in this example) by the annual interest rate of 12 percent. Doing so yields:

Annual Interest = $4,000 x .12 = $480

Annual Operating Costs. You can determine the average annual operating costs by computing the average of the individual annual operating costs. In this example, they are estimated to be $8,000, $8,200, $8,400, and $8,600. The average for these figures is $8,300 which you obtain as follows:

Annual operating costs =

$$\frac{\$8,000 + \$8,200 + \$8,400 + \$8,600}{4} = \$8,300$$

Total Average Annual Cost. For the old equipment, the total average annual cost is simply the sum of the calculated average annual cost for: (1) depreciation, (2) interest, and (3) operating expenses. This sum is $10,280, as shown below.

Item Average-annual cost
Depreciation $1,500
Interest 480
Operating Costs 8,300
 ———
Total $10,280

The New Equipment

Look now at the facts on a piece of new equipment which may be a replacement for the old equipment. The first cost of this new equipment is $30,000. Its life is estimated to be ten years, and it will probably have a salvage value of $6,000. Operating costs with this equipment are expected to average $5,200 a

QUALITY ASSURANCE GUIDE

year. Furthermore, it is estimated to have an annual revenue advantage of $300 over the old equipment. The cost of money is 12 percent per year.

You use the same approach as you did for the old equipment to determine the total average annual cost of this new equipment.

Annual Depreciation Expense. You start with the average annual depreciation expense and find it to be $2,400, as follows:

Annual depreciation =

$$\frac{\$30,000 - \$6,000}{10} = \$2,400$$

Annual Interest Expense. You multiply the average investment in this asset by the interest rate to obtain the average annual interest expense. The average investment is $18,000 (one-half of the sum of the $30,000 first cost and the $6,000 salvage value). The average annual interest expense is $2,160 obtained as follows:

Annual interest = .5 ($30,000 + $6,000) x .12 = $2,160

Total Average Annual Cost. When you also take the estimated operating costs and revenue advantage into account, you find the total average annual cost to be $9,460, as shown below.

Item Average - annual cost
Depreciation $2,400
Interest 2,160
Operating Costs 5,200

_____

$9,760

Less: Revenue advantage 300

_____

$9,460

The Comparison

When you have the total average annual cost for the old and the new equipment, you are ready to compare the two. In the example, the calculated annual cost is $10,280 for the old equipment and $9,460 for the new. On the surface, the new equipment is more economical than the old. But is it?

You may argue that with the old equipment you are committing yourself for only four years, whereas with the new, your commitment is for ten years. This fact suggests a need for considering the kind of equipment that may be available for replacement purposes four years from now as compared with ten years from now.

But no one can forecast that far into the future. It is best to ignore the nature of future replacements in your computations and assume that the replacement available four years from now will have the same annual cost as the one available ten years from now.

Irreducible Factors

When your calculated annual costs show that the one unit of equipment has a decided advantage over the other, you can usually select the better alternative by comparing these calculated costs. But what do you do when the annual costs of the old and the new equipment do not differ greatly? In such a case, you should consider the fact that the estimates might contain errors and that there are things on which a dollar value cannot be placed.

So you may have to base your decision on irreducible factors - factors that cannot be reduced to dollars and cents.

A few examples will suggest the nature of such factors.

First, if total average annual costs are about the same, you will probably favor the equipment that required the smaller investment and has the shorter life. The same will hold true when you suspect that technological advances will result in more efficient equipment becoming available in the near future.

As another example, you will prefer the equipment which has greater output capacity, safety, and reliability even though the value of these is unknown.

And finally, when you suspect that interest rates and the price of new equipment will increase significantly, you will be inclined to invest in new equipment now rather than later.

QUALITY ASSURANCE GUIDE

18. Fixing Production Mistakes

This guide is intended for small manufacturers and deals with the essential issues and steps that should be considered by a manufacturer when a production mistake has been found. A production error is analyzed in check-list form to establish its extent and its effect on the product and the production line and the steps needed for corrective action that integrates the "fix" into the existing production systems and schedules.

What Will You Do?

What would you do if several or several hundred production units manufactured in your plant were found to incorporate a defective or improperly installed component? Assume the logical complication that the defective units had been distributed to numerous work stations along the production line to be fitted into higher assemblies. Add to this the grim fact that defective end items had been shipped from your plant and were now in the transportation pipeline, at your dealers, and in the hands of consumers.

Production mistakes are not unique. To the contrary, they are chronic. They cost industry hundreds of millions of dollars each year, and they waste resources that are becoming increasingly scarce. When you, the manufacturer make a production mistake, we all lose. The ultimate frustration occurs when managers and their people are not sure what needs to be done to correct the problem. When the corrective action process is unorganized or in disarray, the drain on resources is enormous and unpredictable. The ultimate cost of the fix soars.

Production mistakes are a challenge to a good manager's sense of order. Correction is vital to the survival of the company. Actions need to be taken and controlled to reestablish quality production.

The following questions are far from all inclusive. Each product and plant has its own characteristics, and fixing a production mistake would, of necessity, need to be tailored to both. However, the questions and the outline of a corrective action plan should stimulate your thinking and help you to organize your people and resources should you be confronted with a production mistake.

Analysis

1. Do you know the exact physical nature of the

mistake?

Did a part break?

Was a circuit incomplete?

Was an incorrect material used?

Do you know what happened?

2. Have you examined physical evidence of the mistake?

Will a personal examination of the mistake by you help you to understand the problem better?

3. Do you know where in the plant the mistake actually occurred?

Have you pinpointed and brought to the attention of management the specific work unit and work station where the error was first noticed?

Did you track back along the production line to the work station and worker where the mistake was being made?

Did you track the mistake forward along the production system to ascertain the extent to which the fault was included in higher assemblies and end items?

4. Did you stop the work step that was creating the mistake?

5. Did you identify the people, skills, materials, tools and equipment, data or work practices that caused the mistake?

Do you know which were directly responsible?

Do you know which were indirect contributors?

Do you know how they became part of the approved production process?

6. Must you correct the mistake on finished items or on items on which rework would be economically or technologically unprofitable or impractical? In answering this question, have you considered:

Safe use of the final product by the ultimate consumer?

Established quality standards?

The effect on service life?

Maintainability of the part during normal operations?

The effect on the cost of operating the end item?

QUALITY ASSURANCE GUIDE

Other significant characteristics included in the specifications?

7. If the error will not cause significant deviations from drawings or specifications, should you review the situation with the ordering agencies or companies before taking any further action on those items that now incorporate the defect?

8. Should you impose a work stoppage?

Do you know what the effects of a work stoppage will be on:

Your production line?

Your contractual commitments?

Do you have alternate workloads that can be readily injected into the gaps until a corrective action decision for the mistake can be implemented?

9. Have parts, assemblies or end items, incorporating the error, been shipped from your plant? If they have:

Have you estimated the effects of the mistake on the market place?

Have you estimated the effects of a decision to

recall the defective items from your customers, dealers or consumers?

Are trucks or freight cars now being loaded by your shipping department with items that contain the production error?

Should the shipments be off-loaded?

Have you issued instructions to cover the situation?

Have you confirmed that your instructions were complied with?

Do you know the effect of the stop shipment order on the customers scheduled to receive the items?

Do they have sufficient stocks on hand that do not contain the mistake to tide them over the rework period?

Can you identify all shipments of the items that have the production error, by customers' identity, shipping order number, item serial numbers, method/date/time of shipment, and any other means of identification that will assist your customers to locate the faulty items and segregate them from usable stocks in their warehouses, dealers shelves or in actual use?

QUALITY ASSURANCE GUIDE

10. Based on your analysis to this point, should the recipients of items containing the production error be notified?

If notification is to be made, have you issued the required instructions, including the recording of the means of notification, date/time/method, and the names of the persons initiating the contract and receiving the message.

Are you certain the message was received by the customer and understood?

If you have imposed a work stoppage on the production line, and stopped further shipments of the items, do you know your shipping commitments for the next 24 hours, 48 hours, 72 hours?

Should the recipients of the shipping commitments in (the preceding question) be notified of the delay in shipping and given a new shipping date?

11. If the faulty items are to be recalled to the plant, can shipments in the pipeline be diverted back?

If they can be, have you arranged for temporary storage space?

As an alternative to recalling the items back to the

plant, can the shipments be completed and arrangements made with your customers for the rework, either by doing it themselves or by contracting out?

As another alternative, can you send technicians from your plant to your customers facility to fix the error?

Have you examined the alternatives to correct defective items that were shipped and arrived at the most logical and practicable course of action considering your customer's needs, the time factors involved, the economics of the situation, and your reputation?

Do you know what the effects will be of your decision to fix or not to fix?

Taking Action

1. If the mistake is to be fixed, do you know what needs to be done to develop the corrective action and put it into effect?

2. Have you considered the demands that will be made on and the availability of:

Plant facilities (structural and environmental)

Finances?

Energy sources?

Communications systems?

Transportation?

Public relations and Marketing?

Shop equipment?

Materials?

Supplies?

Tools?

Data?

People (skills, training, safety, workhours, etc.)?

Other services?

3. Can the faulty items be processed economically for teardown to get at the error and then re-injected into your routine production system without disrupting the production flow?

If not, do you need a special, one-time production group to do the teardown, repair and reasembly job?

If, after teardown, the parts can be re-injected into routine production, have you identified the points along the production system where each identifiable part or partial assembly can be inserted?

4. Have you identified all the work units and work stations that will be directly affected by the rework of the faulty items and the corrective action in general?

Do you know how they will be affected?

Do the supervisors and direct workers of those work units and at those work stations understand the problem and what is expected of them?

Have you ascertained which work units or work stations can be by-passed during the fix to minimize disruption to normal production and reduce the ultimate cost impact?

5. Will the fix make it necessary to:

Realign work space?

Move shop equipment?

Modify tools and equipment

Fabricate jigs and special holding devices?

Redesign parts?

Revise procedures?

Change standards?

Retrain people?

Reschedule and Reprogram?

Modify contracts with customers?

6. Can the corrective action taken as a result of finding this error be applied to future designs, management practices and production system improvements anywhere else in the plant?

Has this experience given you ideas to improve your operations?

General Characteristics of a Corrective Action Plan

A corrective action should be planned out and integrated into your production control system, which could be Gantt Charting (a bar chart) or the Critical Path Method (a graphic model). Both systems aid production planning and scheduling by setting up time schedules for starting and finishing various tasks on one or many items. Your corrective action plan form requires careful completion according to the following nine steps:

1) Problem: A concise statement of the problem. References can be included to identify other documents giving more detailed information.

2) Work Unit (Prime): The title or other identifying symbol of the shop, unit or group where the cause of the problem exists and where the action will be taken. A mistake may be quite extensive and the effects fragmented and widespread. Actions may be needed by several work units. A sub-plan may be appropriate for the different work units, functions or locations.

3) Work Unit (Associated): The prime work unit usually needs help from other units. It may be useful to identify these supporting units, their supervisors and telephone numbers. It can save time for those directly involved in the action.

4) Date: The date the plan was approved can provide a valuable control device. The plan may need to be revised to include additional steps, delete certain actions, or change procedures even as the action proceeds. The DATE plus a note that the sheet supersedes one of a prior DATE is the control.

The next three Blocks represent the Task Breakdown. It may be more logical to break the actions down by work station; worker in some situations; in other cases the "Start/Completion Date" may be the most important factor in sequencing the steps. Circumstances may dictate that accessibility to certain parts on the assembly compels the sequence. Each situation and set of circumstances would need to be analyzed in detail to arrange the best sequence.

5) Work Station/Responsible Worker: Who does what, and in what sequence? The station and worker should he in the WORK UNIT identified at the top of the page.

6) Operations: To the most practicable extent this space should state the specific actions that needed to be taken-sequentially if possible. Generalizations should he avoided as they might be subjected to varying interpretations and lead to confusion. This should not be the place to say why the mistake happened or otherwise analyze the problem. This space should confine itself to do-this type instructions. It should be of DIRECT use to the worker doing the job.

7) Starting /Completion Dates: The dates should be realistic, otherwise, a work stoppage could occur. The dates should consider such diverse factors as the availability of tools and equipment, test sets, raw materials, energy, skills, workhours and work shifts. It could consider whether or not the dates would be compatible with normal production operations. If new design or fabrication techniques are to be applied, the starting dates could be affected accordingly. A START and COMPLETION date would ordinarily be required for each entry under OPERATIONS.

8) Follow-Up Date: Follow-up is an option of management to assure that the action was taken and was adequate. It could include examining the product, checking documentation or interviews with the people doing the work. It assures the manager that the job was done, and done right.

9) Confirm Permanent Correction: After the crisis has passed, management may wish to take that extra step that would prevent the mistake from recurring. What really caused the problem? What should be done about it? Is a permanent change needed in tools, equipment or materials? Should the shop layout be changed? Do workers need additional

training? What about quality control and product inspection procedures? The fact that a mistake occurred in one unit could mean that it might happen in another. The mistake that was corrected could provide an opportunity for a significant technical or management improvement throughout the plant.

Appendix: Special Free Bonuses

You can access your free bonuses here:

https://www.bizmove.com/bizgifts.htm

Here's what you get:

#1 How to Be a Good Manager and Leader; 120 Tips to improve your Leadership Skills (Leadership Video Guide).

Learn how to improve your leadership skills and become a better manager and leader. Here's how to be the boss people want to give 200 percent for. In this video you'll discover 120 powerful tips and strategies to motivate and inspire your people to bring out the best in them.

#2 Small Business Management: Essential Ingredients for Success (eBook Guide)

Discover scores of business management tricks, secrets and shortcuts. This Ebook guide does far more than impart knowledge - it inspires action.

#3 How to Manage Yourself for Success; 90 Tips to Better Manage Yourself and Your Time (Self Management Video Guide)

You are responsible for everything that happens in your life. Learn to accept total responsibility for yourself. If you don't manage yourself, then you are letting others have control of your life. In this video you'll discover 90 powerful tips and strategies to better manage yourself for success.

#4 80 Best Inspirational Quotes for Success (Motivational Video Guide)

For this video we scanned thousands of motivational and inspirational quotes to bring you this collection of the best 80 motivational quotes for success in life.

#5 Top 10 Habits to Adopt From Highly Successful People (Self Growth Video Guide)

In this video you'll discover the top 10 habits of highly successful people that you can adopt and achieve success in your life.

#6 Personal Branding: How to Make a Killer First Impression (Self Promotion Video Guide)

This video deals with personal branding. While promoting your personal brand, you'll discover in this video the ten most effective things you can do to make the best first impression possible.

#7 How to Advance Your Career 10 Times Faster (Career Advancement Video Guide)

The most important thing to remember about your

career today is that you need to be responsible for your own future. In this video you'll discover 10 powerful strategies to advance your career faster.

#8 How to Get Success in Life; 10 Strategies to Attract the Life You Want (Self Actualization Video Guide)

To have more, we must be more of who we are. The secret is in the doing; none of it matters until we do something about it. In this video you'll discover 10 powerful strategies to attract the life you want.

#9 A Comprehensive Package of Business Tools

Here's a collection featuring dozens of business related templates, worksheets, forms, and plans; covering finance, starting a business, marketing, business planning, sales, and general management.

#10 People Management Skills: How to Deal with Difficult Employees (Managing People Video Guide)

Problem behavior on the part of employees can erupt for a variety of reasons. In this video you'll discover the top ten ideas for dealing with difficult employees.

www.ingramcontent.com/pod-product-compliance
Lightning Source LLC
Chambersburg PA
CBHW070817220526
45466CB00002B/692